WHAT I APPRECIATE ABOUT MY TEACHER

To:

_____

From:

_____

I **appreciate** you. You don't just teach the children. You help **prepare** kids for the **road** ahead in life.

You **deserve** a break.

Because of you,
I've come to
love_____

I remember, when
I came to your class
I was not able to

_____

but now

_____

Your **sacrifices** don't go **unnoticed**. Your extra work **means** a lot to me.

You've **made** a positive **difference** in my life.

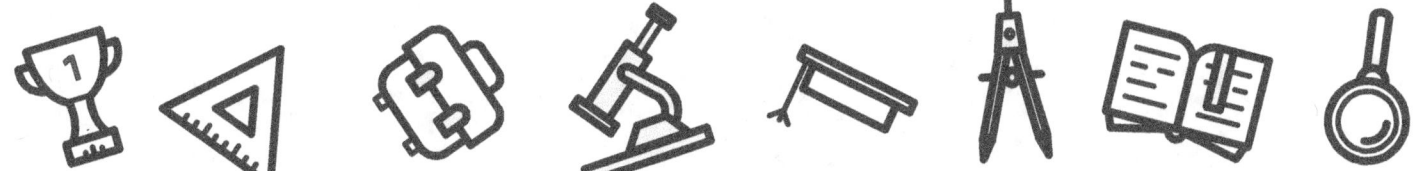

I'll keep in my heart all your positive words like

_____

Because of you,
I want to become

_____

I never **forgot** this one thing you **said** to me. I am **happy** the **words** didn't go in one ear and out the other.

You **saw** something in me that I didn't see in **myself.**

Just you, in your kindness, knew that today I'll be able to

_____

To

_____

_____

_____

_____

_____

I will **use** the skills
you **taught** me.

You're the reason
I **accomplished** this.

I remember when I

_____

and you

_____

You always have had kind words for me when I was sad, like

_____

I **seriously** think you're the **funniest** teacher I've **ever** had.

I was so **excited** to come in your class **everyday**.

I remember when I

_____

and you

_____

I liked all

_____

I was amazed by

_____

and I was excited when

_____

Just **wanted** to let you know I **appreciate** all the **hard work** you're putting into your **classroom**.

I'll never **forget** you.

You will forever remain
in my mind like this

And not just on reading and writing but

_____

_____

_____

Thank you for your **patience** throughout this year. It **meant** the world to me.

Your **positivity** and **encouragement** brightened my days.

I was excited every morning to step into your class and see

_____

and hear

_____

and feel

_____

You game the strength I needed to take the next steps towards my dream of

_____

You really **captured** my interest with daily l**essons**.

Thank you for **emboldening** me.

I never thought I would

_____

YOU DID IT!!!

I like

_____

_____

_____

Your **kindness**
made me feel
welcomed and
comfortable.

As a **super hero** your strength lies in your **heart**, your **eyes** and your **voice.**

Your smile and your words have lifted me higher than I dreamed

_____

When it comes
to your students,
nothing can stop
you believe.

_____

This was a **tough** year, but **you got me** through it!

You are, **hands down**, the **best teacher** I've ever had.

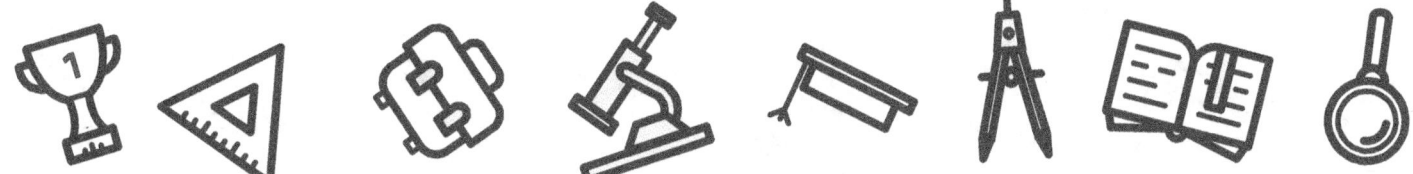

The most amazing thing you taught me is

_____

_____

Thank you! This is my present for you

You **inspired** me to begin this **new chapter** in my life. I couldn't have **done** it **without you**.

Thank you for your hard work. It's work I could never do let alone do so well. I appreciate your gift and feel lucky that my child has you as a teacher.

You are the best
team player!
I trusted you

_____

_____

Notes

Notes

_____
_____
_____
_____
_____
_____
_____
_____
_____
_____
_____
_____
_____
_____
_____
_____
_____
_____

Notes

_____

_____

_____

_____

_____

_____

_____

_____

_____

_____

_____

_____

_____

_____

_____

_____

_____

_____

_____

Notes

_____
_____
_____
_____
_____
_____
_____
_____
_____
_____
_____
_____
_____
_____
_____
_____
_____
_____